CENTER STAGE

7 Sparkling Solos that Showcase the Talents
of the Late Elementary Pianist

☆ MARTHA MIER ☆

The seven solos in *Center Stage,* Book 1, were written to high-
light the pianistic abilities of young pianists. These solos are
ideal for performance at school talent shows, recitals, or for
sharing with friends and family.

Most of the pieces in Book 1 are original compositions. One
solo is an arrangement of familiar folk songs of America, thus
enhancing the appeal of this collection to audiences.

Showcase your talents with the exciting and spirited solos
from *Center Stage,* Book 1!

Martha Mier

American Folk Medley 14
Country Jamboree 12
Down by the Bayou 8
Hometown Parade 6
Midnight Capers 2
Purple Pinwheels 4
Under the Big Top 10

Copyright © MMII by Alfred Publishing Co., Inc.
All rights reserved. Printed in USA.
ISBN 0-7390-2786-7

Midnight Capers

Martha Mier

Mysteriously

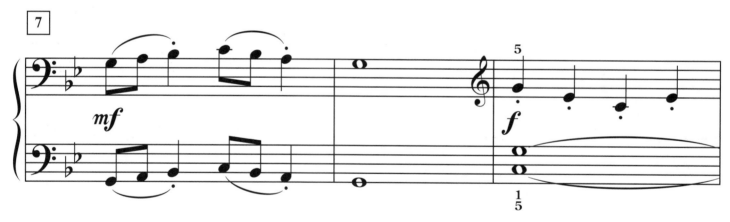

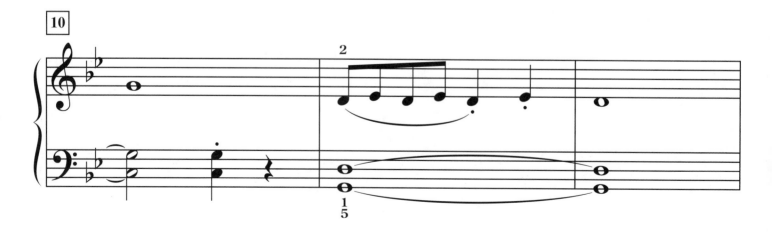

Purple Pinwheels

Martha Mier

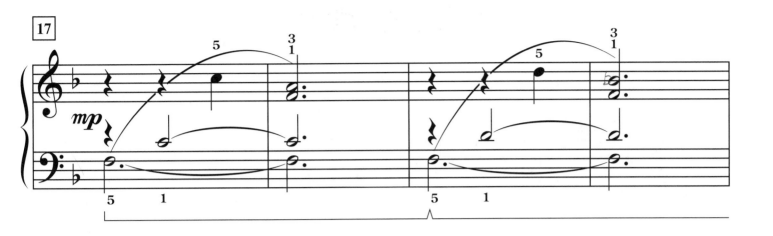

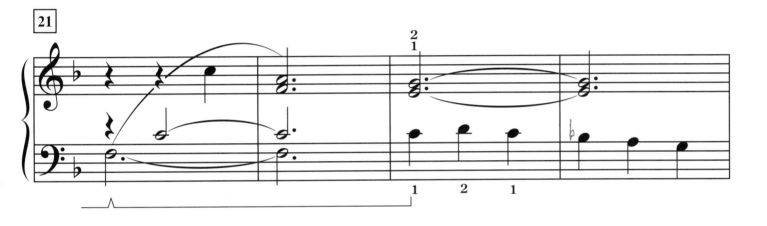

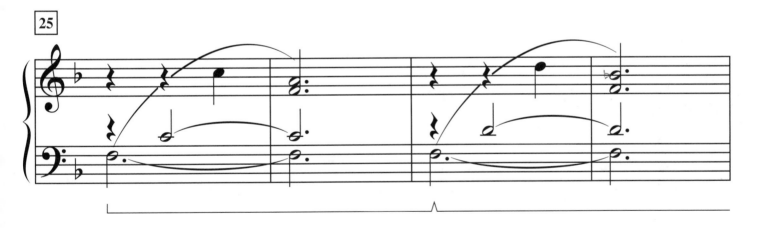

Hometown Parade

Martha Mier

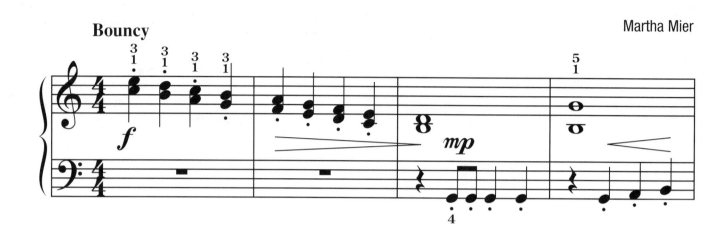

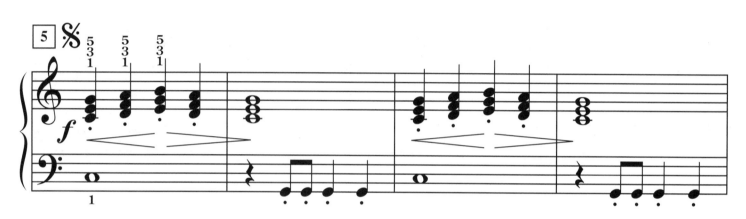

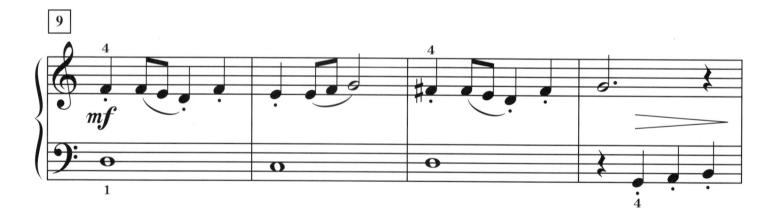

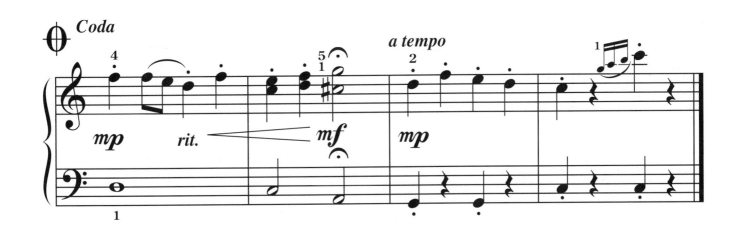

Down by the Bayou

Martha Mier

Under the Big Top

Martha Mier

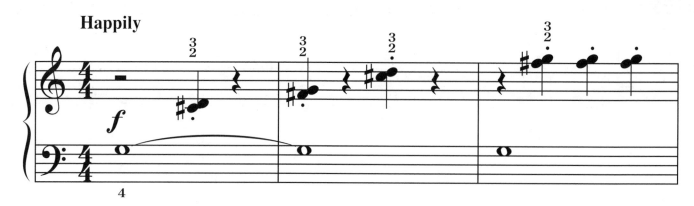

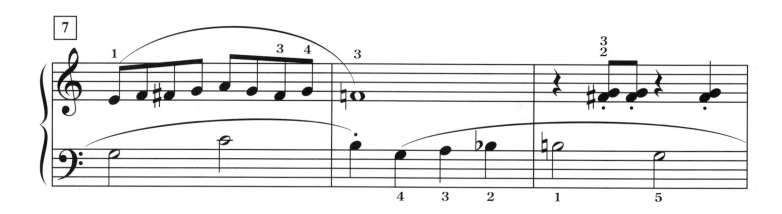

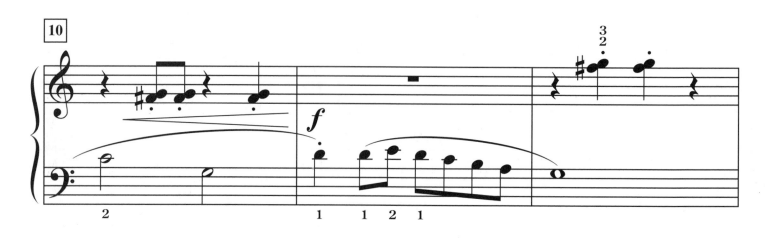

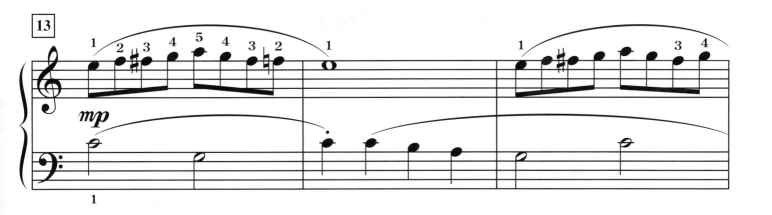

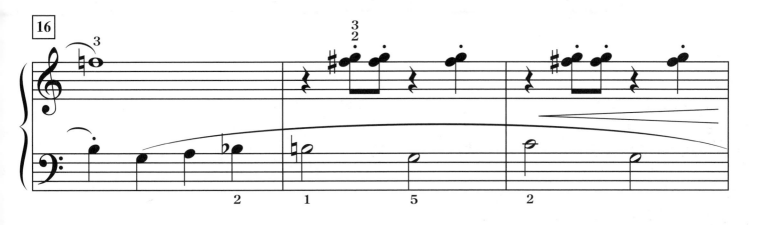

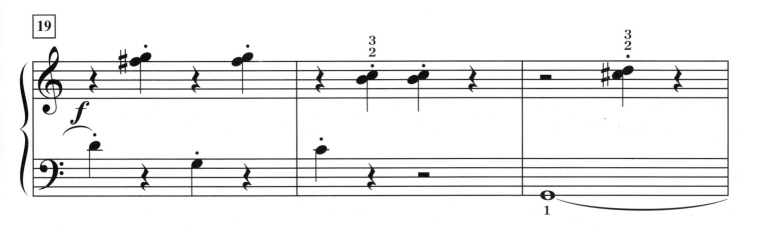

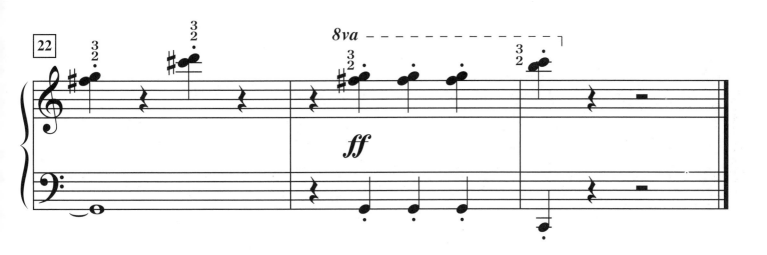

Country Jamboree

Martha Mier

American Folk Medley

Arr. by Martha Mier

With spirit

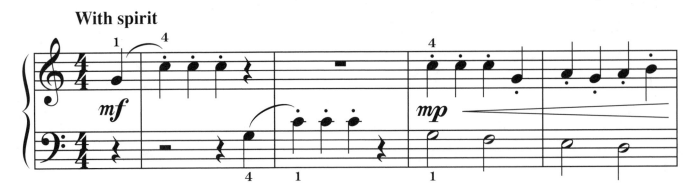

5 *Old MacDonald Had a Farm*

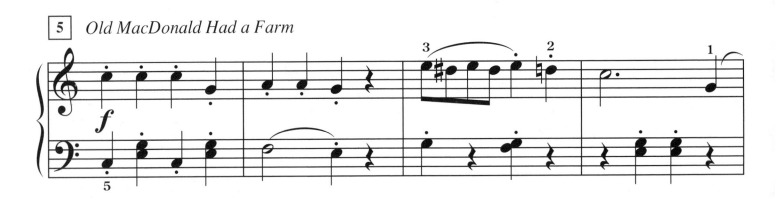

9

13

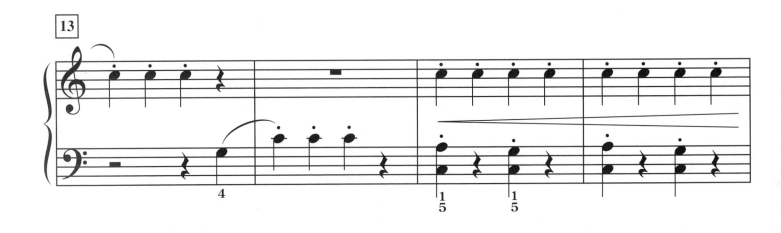

Oh! Susannah
Both hands
8va - - -

37

Tempo primo

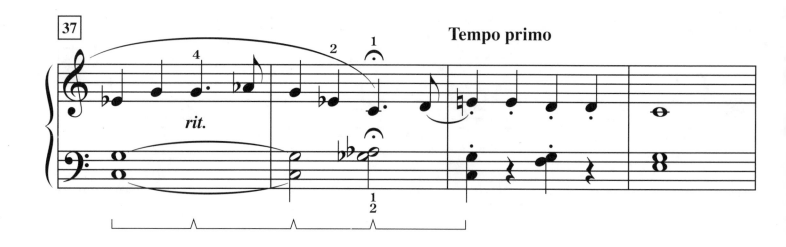

41

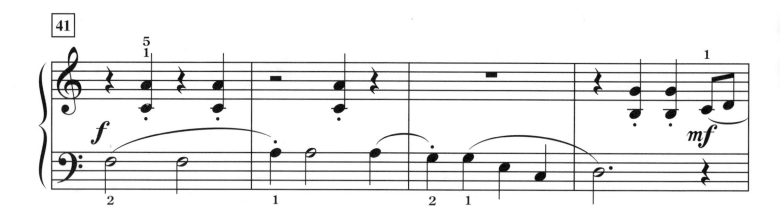

45

49

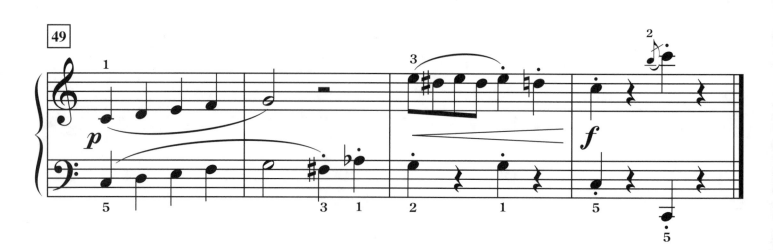